Lombardi Voices

VOLUME 21   WINTER 2024

A Publication of the Georgetown Lombardi Arts and Humanities Program

Dear Readers:

When I was asked to introduce this year's *Lombardi Voices,* my thoughts went to my colleague Michelle Berberet's Expressive Writing workshops and the other arts programs offered by The Georgetown Lombardi Arts & Humanities Program. These artistic spaces, both in the hospital and online, connect us and build community. I've found writing to be particularly useful for bringing people together.

Opportunities to form human connections seem to be especially important these days. Recently, officials across the globe have warned about an epidemic of loneliness and isolation. In 2023, U.S. surgeon general Vivek H. Murthy released an **advisory** calling loneliness, isolation and lack of connection a public health crisis. That same year, the WHO established the **Commission on Social Connection** that is working to make dealing with loneliness a global public health priority.

Addressing the crisis of loneliness will require vigorous action across all sectors of society, including the arts. **Research** suggests that writing, especially in community, can be a useful tool for meaningful connection.

Throughout my life, I have used writing, both as a writer and active listener, to build relationships with friends and loved ones. It has helped us grow closer even through times of grief and loss.

Poet and writer, Pat Schneider taught me about the community building potential of writing. For several years, I wrote with her and members of our community in workshops she taught in her house in Amherst, Massachusetts. In her book, *"Writing Alone and With Others",* she writes, "When we write, we create, and when we offer our creation to one another, we close the wound of loneliness and may participate in healing the broken world."

Not long after I first attended Pat's workshops, I began working in the Arts and Health Field. During the roughly 15 years I've spent facilitating writing and art making in healthcare settings, I have worked with patients, caregivers and medical students, all of whom used the creative arts to express themselves. I continue to experience the community building capabilities of the writing community as a writer-in-residence with the AHP. The ongoing legacy of *Lombardi Voices* is testament to that.

I hope these poems will inspire you. Many of them began in Michelle's Expressive Writing classes, so it only makes sense for the last words to be hers, "Writing together and sharing our words connects us because we find out we are not alone."

Warm regards,

Dylan Klempner
AHP Artist-in-Residence

Table of Contents

74 Lost in Mind- Mohamed Adde.................................. 6

The Stuff of My Life- Christine Anderson........................... 7

Advice To Writers- Rose Avent....................................... 8

The Well of Wisdom Deep- Zairi Aymen...................... 9

Your Space- Joanne Bekkerus................................... 10

It Begins- Britta Benson... 11

Universal Eloquence- Nora Bertognotti..................... 13

Lego City: Instructions- Jean Biegun....................... 14

I Woke?- Gloria Birdsall... 16

Nyx- Mayurakshi Chaturvedi.................................. 17

Beauty- Gayle Danley.. 18

Early January- Andrea Cecile Davila........................ 20

Farewell- Sally Ferenschak..................................... 22

The Wildflower Field- Christine Ford....................... 23

Standing Up Again- Preethi Govindaraj................... 24

Seasons of Contrast- Marjorie Young Grays.............. 25

Mentor- Bill Greene.. 27

But Still We Can Dream- Kirsten Hughson............... 29

A Healer's Polarity- Anthony Hyatt......................... 30

The Hotel Room- Mirta Imperatori.......................... 31

Metastatic Prostate Cancer Haiku- Bob Jacobs.......... 32

RBG- Judy Thibault Klevins.................................... 33

Magic- Hiram Larew.. 34

Torn Hero- Richard Lee.. 35

Grace- Reb Cantor Lisa Levine................................ 36

Architecture 2.0- Alison Lewis................................ 37

Resilience- Margaret Marrello.................................. 41

Existence while hoping for a cure- M.S. Marquart...... 42

This Is What You Get- Mora Lee Mattern.................. 44

Goodbye My Sweet Boy- Grace May.................................. 46

Our Poem- Elissa Mitman.. 47

Intergenerational Healing- Carrie Monger............................ 48

Back to Water- Jim Soon Moon... 51

Stretching and Moving- Carren Oler................................... 52

En Plein Air- Helen Pagowska.. 54

You Are Complete- Josephine Palmieri................................. 55

Churches Say Amen!- Lauren Poteat.................................... 56

An Ancient, Lost Language- Lynn Quinn.............................. 57

The Background- Stacee Ryan... 58

Reply All- Kristen Sheely... 60

Life in the Folds- Samantha Simons.................................... 63

Life's Music- Donna M. St. John.. 64

Sun- Jack Tattersal... 65

Frosty Night- Connie Taylor.. 69

Lately- Sara Gómez Trillos... 69

Whispering Words On The Wind- Kathy Why........................ 72

Draw Breath-Mag. Judith Wurzinger................................. 73

74 Lost In Mind

Mohamed Adde

My body is present but my mind is gone like a soul leaving the body. This is where the excitement comes in. Funny when I think of excitement, I think of full of life. Excitement should not be your typical scenario, also not dead body. In a way excitement can be imagination, thinking, and wondering happiness. A world deprived of excitement is a world with no imagination.

The Stuff of My Life

Christine Anderson

A flower, a blade of grass
moving in a summer breeze
blue skies and white fluffy clouds
and the swaying of trees

Nature has an elegance
even on a bad weather day
it's passionate stirrings
deliver crashing waves into the bay

The soft breeze, delicate as a feather
lands like a sigh on my hot skin
calming my mind, soothing my heart
and nourishing from within

Advice to Writers

Rose Avent

Don't think about
laundry lumped in the hamper or
mending lingering in the basket by the door.

Don't fret about
soup simmering on the stove or
chard waiting to be chopped for dinner.

Forget emails.
Ignore the bills.

It's Summer! Step outside.
Wriggle your grass-gentled toes in morning dew
allow your plans to sail away like kites on the wind.

Anticipate sun's nourishment
inhale all this green glorious light
straight into your soul.

Then drag your chair under the tallest shade tree
sketch a poem of bird song and
a prayer of gratitude for this
lush and luminous summer day.

The Well of Wisdom Deep

Zairi Aymen

In a realm where whispers waltz and wisdom thrives,
Lies a timeless dance of elegance and life.
A tapestry woven with threads of grace,
A symphony of souls in an eternal embrace.
Life, a painter with a palette so wide,
Brushstrokes bold and tender side by side.
In every hue, a lesson, a tale, a fall
A journey through winds, through calm and gale.
In the quietude of a starlit night,
Elegance dances in the pale moonlight.
So here's to the dance, to the beauty we weave,
To the moments of grace in which we believe.
For in elegance and life, a truth we find,
A melody of peace for the heart and mind.
Let us drink from the well of wisdom deep,
Where the seeds of love and kindness sleep.
For in the dance of Eloquence and life,
Lies the strength to endure, to overcome strife.

Your Space

Joanne Bekkerus

Reside in this space, your space.
It's where you sit silently,
Pondering all that drifts by.
The movement is soft, quiet,
On the rhythmic warm currents
Of the extensive cosmos.
Driven onward by a rich,
Compassionate, graceful breeze.
Existing in a deep blue
Heavenly ocean of time.
This is where the second hand
Observes a simple, loose count.
Here discovery is made.
Remember that space, your space.

It begins

Britta Benson

It begins
with a shiver,
that first feeble inkling
of something you know
without knowing
and you've always known this
since before.

It begins
with a tingle
of finding,
of falling,
of choosing to pause
and hold
that cold stubborn thing
in your soul
a little longer,
a little looser,
without judgment,
without grudge,
without any preconception.

You are not this.
You are not that.
You are not what you thought you would be.

It begins
when you allow
yourself
to stop and stare
in open wonder
at what you truly are,
here,
now,
perhaps wonky,
perhaps wobbly,
perhaps weak,
but,
oh,
so,
YOU!

This is the moment.

It begins.

Call it recognition.
Call it remembrance.
I call it love.

UNIVERSAL ELOQUENCE

Nora Bertognotti

When an arpeggio stirs up memories
When in a single note, a melody incites tears
When an emotional song tugs on your heartstring
That is universal eloquence!

Music is the most moving and powerful medium of expression
Dare to dive into the intense finesse of Franco Piersanti's *"Tenderness"*
Feel the compassionate lament of John Newton's *"Amazing Grace"*
What a delight!

Then, try to perceive the thrill of the refreshing continuity of
"The Moldau" river of Bedřich Smetana
While in Vienna, dance to Shostakovich's *"The Second Waltz,"*
What astounding elegance!

Sing along with Joaquín Rodrigo's *"Concierto de Aranjuez"*
and be swept away to paradise by the melancholy melody
Receive the excitement of Vivaldi's *"Four Seasons,"* which overflows
us
with jubilation and wonder.
Absolute happiness!

LEGO City: Instructions

Jean Biegun

1

Start with an altar on a green baseplate.
Use light and dark gray bricks for stones.
Stack several round single-dot pieces to make candles.
Top each with a little flame (Item No: 37775).
Attach to the altar.

2

Build two high structures—totems, columns, or steles
to mark the area for awe.
Assemble three torches taller than the candles.
Finish them with larger flames (Item No: 28618)
to light the path on moonless nights.

3

Pick a minifigure without a hat
and nothing in its circular gripping hands.
Bend it to a bow.
Secure it to the baseplate in front of the altar.

4

In an empty corner, construct a room of four walls.
Create a rectangular portal in one.
Place in the room another bare-headed minifigure
singularly smiling widely.
Guide it through the opening.
Let it disappear for a while.

5

On an adjacent beige baseplate,
connect different blues, grays, whites, and browns
to form a river of forgiveness.
Make it look muddy in sections
where regrets soak.

6

Design a busy street next to the water
with speeding cars and bustling mini figures grasping
objects, their identifying hats on their heads.
Noise. Make noise sound effects here.

7

Choose two of the hurrying figures.
Help them step away from the road,
release their hats and held things.
Move them into the river along its flow.

8

Gently lift the little people onto the shore
to rest by a tree anchored there.
Then lead them across to the green baseplate,
to the stone altar where
with relief and deep breaths
they too bend and bow.

I Woke?

Gloria Birdsall

I woke in a state of flux

I woke in a way I'd never done before

The imminent danger felt real

The imminent sense of civil war

The pain was immense to the point of a sharp cry of no return

The pain was a shock to the system, so would I die?

No answer came upon my lips

No answer from the radio, TV or X was ready to relieve me

I sank back into my pillow in readiness

I sank into a mindless, physical and spiritual delusional state

Was this the return of Jesus our Saviour;

Was this when earth came to an end as we all knew it?

.............................fullstop

Nyx

Mayurakshi Chaturvedi

On a warm windy night, I saw you, in full form,
blowing like a stormy wind, under the setting moon.
Your eyes gleamed, heralding the beginning of secrets,
which would destroy me from within.
I know how you did it, how you brought me to my knees,
sent me down a strange spiral that destroyed my soul.
I wish I had the courage to stop myself,
but it was too delicious not to give in.
The silver pen shone in the pale moonlight,
and the red ink flowed into the darkness of the night,
as the distant songs, and murmurs, faded away.
When I lay my heart at your feet, my skin was bare,
and nothing felt like anything I had ever known,
as you grasped my face in your stone-cold hands.
I had hoped I would be lost in time,
not know what happened to me,
yet here I am, my skin still bare.
I feel maybe I could be a stormy wind
Blowing across the things I know, and also the things you taught me.
Whether that was before I had lived, or after,
I forget.
But I have been transformed forever,
and I now know what was at stake before I came into being,
and what remains long after I am done.

Beauty

Gayle Danley

I have to keep telling myself **Beauty**

Look   there it is   there it was   there it will be

When I touch the cream face of a dandelion wanting to blow but instead hold her close to my heart

Beauty

When me and Noah lie down at night, he whispers

"I'm so glad you're my mama. If you die before me, I'll visit your grave every day, saying thank you mommy thank you mommy."

Waves lick their lips folding into themselves

Dying/reborn

Hum of sunlight praying over my legs

Beauty

Sedative of song

Fingers spelling love on shoulders

Women who have stood at the foot of my mountains

Watched me fall

Skin scarred

I land in their arms

Over/over

Juice of peaches

gather of raindrops on petals unsuspecting

I must remember these are more than the empty mouths of hotel rooms, gash of bills I cannot pay. How love never showed up at the prom. So many funerals I've made a file folder of obituaries. Sorrow wafting up in me then settling at the base of my spine. I hobble when I walk.

The 6 year old and I have an agreement. If we are ever lost from each other, just remember to go back to where we last were. Love's lesson.

The solace of return.

Beauty

Sometimes I peek over the cliff of my life and cry

Gayle, it's not about the drive, it's about the road, how she reaches for your hands, dusty but at least they're smooth

I always end up where I am going

Beauty:

Murmur of cat

Wind asking trees to dance

My children are all breathing

Bit of bread in the pantry

See those roses rising through dirt, hands made tender by the rock's weight

Beauty

Beauty

Beauty

Early January

Andrea Cecile Davila

for Ace

On the same morning Isa and I walked
across the frozen lake for the first time
the water suddenly not water
but a vast expanse to explore
from a landscape previously
unknown, unavailable

I was startled at the sound
of the wild geese and looked up
to witness those many tight small v's
line up a seam across the sky
together into one large V
pointing their direction home

It was that morning
I unwrapped you
for the first time
getting dizzy with the turning
of your body, confused
and scared
to look at your stitches
those small tight v's
wild geese in the white of your chest
a new landscape
uncharted

On our way back
we noticed footprints
frozen into the snow
made jagged by the wind
"A beast must have made these mama"
Says Isa, about the biggest, most rough-edged ones
that break the smooth surface of the snow-covered ice

Maybe, Isa, or maybe it was
someone working really damn hard
for really damn long
to finally get home.

FAREWELL

Sally Ferenschak

Whither thou Goest
With thee, I Am..
From the Mountains
To the Oceans..
To Countries, Afar…

The Power of Three
From Heavens above..
The Spirit…Inspiration..
Be with You Always..
Every Moment… Every Day..

New Missions Arrive…
New Journeys for Our Lives
Our Friends..
Our World…
Our Beliefs…

Your Wanderings We Honour…
As We Walk to Outreach
Together with You..
Together with Friends..

Whither thou Goest..
Vaya con Dios, My Friend…
Vaya con Dios..
UNTIL
Once more
We Journey Together…
For Our Missions
…Ourselves..
Our World… and Our God..

The Wildflower Field

Christine Ford

The wildflower field

Is spotted like flannel pajamas

Worn soft from many washings

After cold-syrup nights

Of high fever, close covers,

Hands rinsed with Ivory soap

Fluttering to forehead,

Tummy, and back again—

Nights warm with clouds of whispers—

Brother and sister sporting identical pajamas

Spotted with blue cowboys and yellow cowgirls

That after many washings only look like wildflowers in a field.

STANDING UP AGAIN

Preethi R. Govindaraj

I must let you know
How you have helped me grow
to learn to tolerate
The pain and persist,
even if it is slow.
You sensed my uncertainty
and acknowledged my fears
you nudged me on, not
withstanding my tears.
You encouraged my small steps,
while holding the bars
you never stopped trying,
when my hope was sparse.
Only you knew of my journey
Of collapsing at the pinnacle
and turned my calamity,
into a miracle.
No one could envision
the makings of a marvel
an architectural piece
from crumbs and gravel.
With your conviction,
 I held on tightly-
you always trusted me
even when I trudged unwillingly.
Now I can inspire,
Who deal with deformities
to arouse the dormant spirit,
in the face of adversities.
I realize the circle never ends
though one may momentarily stop,
If you choose to stand motionless,
Despondency may fill the gap.

Seasons of Contrast

Marjorie Young Grays

Winter is not my season.

No,

I am sparkling summer sunshine

Loud, explosive as the 4th of July,

Joyous as Juneteenth, and twice as free.

Bursting into your life and every space

As if I owned it

While you, my love, are

silent as a mighty oak

Hidden in an ancient forest.

Rooted in Truth,

Forever wise, and without pretense.

Silent as snowfall

you warmed my heart

With your kind and steady love.

So as I fall to earth

A Starburst spent and fizzling

into glowing embers,

I am restored by the quiet strength

of your embrace.

You my love

are quiet as an ancient forest

still as snowfall and as restful

so when my boisterous blaze has fizzled into

drifting embers,

I am warmed by the quiet strength of your embrace.

Mentor

Bill Greene

I'm in uncharted territory now, for sure.
Without the benefit of chart or compass,
I'm finally left to forage
this final bit alone.

The last of the truly wise men I've known
is slipping from view.
Leaving me without the benefit
of welcomed wisdom or sage advice.

I'm my own mentor now.
Navigating this final field alone,
Wishing I could hear the voices that were so dear to me
just one more time.

I used to have a number of them
dotting my path like fence posts,
Keeping me on the straight and narrow,
Sounding the alarm whenever I veered too far one way or the other.

But now time, age and natural attrition have thinned their ranks,
Leaving that solitary soul who is now being overtaken
by a sad twist of fate…
his strength being his weakness.

Even he would have to laugh at the irony of it.
The strange, cruel way that life
brings you to the inevitable,
The circle finally being broken.

I wish you well old friend.
And I hope this journey proves peaceful and serene.
A final testament to who you were
and will always be to me.

But Still We Can Dream

Kirsten Hughson

dreaming of green

    growing

        warm air

soil   lush   verdant   springy moss

bare feet and fingers digging in soil

    tomato leaves scented hands

    scratchy cucumber vines

    flowers that precede fruit

fat bees buzzing

    peppers from green to red

alive earth awake earth

yet still she slumbers, not yet ready to wake…

but still we can

dream

A Healer's Polarity:
Listening with Boundaries

Anthony Hyatt

I have a feeling that cancer is not just individual.
It affects us as a collective.
Healing can come thru listening to words and their residual.
Arising when the invective yields to the reflective.

I bring the laying on of ears.
The gift of presence,
Sometimes absorbing tears and fears,
That overlie essence.

Knowing there is more than one truth,
In this world uncouth,
I must honor the line,
Between what is yours and what is mine.

Then I must release....
Listen inward,
Rebalance.

Seek again the peace...
Move us toward,
A new dance.

Dissonant melodies need harmony's emergence.
The rhythm is there.
But where is the convergence?
Perhaps in hearts that care.

The Hotel Room

Mirta Imperatori

The hotel room,
Emptiness
Tasting gravity,
Falling.
It's winter
Silhouettes in the snow.
False dreams,
We are pilgrims
Strangers in a foreign land.
Bare walls
Water dripping,
The urgency to get out
Either way we are too close.
The struggles in the darkness
Comings and goings.
We are together for a short time.
Love – the accident.
What is our true fate?
Chaos and complexity,
Then the melancholy.
Both fallen
We dance in our shared silence.
Filling the whole space
Sparks of light.
But fallen from grace.
Can't explain the attraction,
We are alive and destroying our lives
Back again in this bare hotel room.

Metastatic Prostate Cancer Haiku

Bob Jacobs

Several Rogue Cells
Bent On Taking Me Over
NOT GONNA HAPPEN

RBG

Judy Thibault Klevins

The handsome men
Arrive at the theatre
An hour before the show

Plastic devices in their ears
They scan the space
Like eagles

Then, smiling, they
Gather the ushers
Briefing them on
Their duties

A few minutes
Right before the play begins
RBG arrives

The audience stops
Moving and schmoozing
And becomes
Quietly respectful

At intermission
The eagles continue
Their silent scans
From places where they could see
Everyone and where everyone knew
They were watching

The performance ends
She is gone
Before we know it

Magic

Hiram Larew

This poem first appeared in *Orbis*.

The stars in your chest --
  the sounds of their glow
  their flash blink wings
  their touch top skies.

These leaps towards light --
  these grateful urging holy stars
  in your chest and now in your throat.

Their voices of beams
  even into your heart and beyond.

Their blaze --
  each star that starts in your chest
  and spins out from there.

Spins you as nothing else can
  as magic comes true
  with your chances so inside and out.

With each and every star
  so over the moon.

Torn Hero

Richard Lee

I could've sworn
That I wasn't broken and torn
Getting hit by the bull's horn
This feeling is foreign

Somehow I managed to live
Couldn't spare what to give
Deep end that I dive
I also managed to survive

I manage to piece together
Last an impact, Last forever
Echoing throughout the generation
Anxiousness in my bones with hesitation

Got to make that ripple
To make that wave
Before I become cripple
There's alot that I gave

Grace

Reb Cantor Lisa Levine

Grace means accepting a gift
and saying thank you.
Grace means accepting a compliment
when you believe you've underachieved.
Grace means smiling
even when your heart is breaking.
Grace means rising above something
that makes you uncomfortable.
Grace means opening your heart
and allowing judgments to dissipate.
Grace means acceptance
of things not within your control.
Grace means keeping an optimistic countenance
even when the darkest of clouds threaten.
Grace means turning the other cheek
and believing everything will turn out okay.
Grace is having hope when hope seems lost.
I pray that grace will surround us
in protective love
allowing us to walk
through our day
with a smile on our faces
in our eyes and in our hearts.
So that joy might prevail.

Architecture 2.0

Alison Lewis

Start where you are,
With who you are.
Your brand of wondrous, unexpected, breathtaking Lego pieces!
Your original building blocks.

Right where you stand,
Yes, right there, on that spot,
Rough ground, or not
Stable, or highly polished
Blocks that fit,
Or don't seem to at all...
Until they do.

You can begin
to
Build
What you have dreamed & hoped & longed for,
What you have always imagined,
And,
never entertained.

Every building project,
Begins with a thought in mind,
A vision in heart.

Your deeply lovely
Infrastructure,
Will guide you,
if you let it,
when you trust it.
Foundation has a language of its own,

That insists on being seen and heard.
Where does yours lie?
Is it elegant?
sometimes yes...maybe not.
But eloquent...
Absolutely,
Unquestioningly!

What you have been building,
Will speak and speak,
And surprise...
even you,
Perhaps, especially you
in some moments!

Is what you have built,
what was imagined?
Big picture true?
But maybe with raw materials other than those you first conceived?

Sometimes the build is interrupted,
Left unfinished,
at least for now, for a time.

Sometimes we want to, need to,
get to,
Re-envision the build,
though not always by choice,
[meaning our choice].
Sometimes life deals the hand,
And what seemed complete,
as good as it would get,
Must be dismantled...
A thousand dominos cascading!

That is where your scaffolding can show up and do its job,
needed...
until it is no longer.

Unexpected does not have to be bad,
and
A detour can still lead to destiny.

There are so many things that are part of Life's build:
Homes and roads
Fences and bridges,
Skyscrapers and tunnels,
Furniture and walls...
Reputation,
and
Legacy ~

And what about your treehouse?
Did it ever get built,
Can it still be built...
with brand new blueprints?

Your difference,
made by your presence,
by the choice that you made
To show up in your life
and in the world.
Yes!
Your difference...
That is how a life gets built.

It happens,
With every material chosen
And all the layers that are forged.
Constructing parts, creating a design

You have strengthened and established,
Dug deep
and raised up!
You caused it to prosper,
Sometimes against formidable odds.

~

Standing where I do,

I want you to know that
I think,
That you are
A [Master] Builder
And I hope that you will Love that about yourself!

Your love letter...
To receive as gift to yourself
To share,
To be proud of,
[If you dare!]

For the house
that you have built ~

Resilience

Margaret Marrelio

Ferocious and rapturous
She embodies the shore.
Sparkles of reflection
bowed us in.
Our feet scorched in sand,
welcomed her cool touch.

We scrambled to beat her breakers,
Buoyed by victories.
She mocked our boldness.
In fury took me hostage.

I felt hands
tighten around my suit straps.
Pull me out of her grip.
I gasped for air.
Again she hurdled towards us.
Lifted into her arms,
rising into the sky, a swell in the distance.
I grabbed my mother's extended hand.
We climbed the next wave, then another and another.

Existence while hoping for a cure (#MillionsMissing)

M.S. Marquart

Lying on the couch in a somnolent twilight,
the same days repeat,
over and over.

Ever a tyrant, my ME/CFS
dictates only watching television I've already seen before.
My brain fog commands no distress from trying to keep up
with plot points. My anxiety insists on no nerves over whether characters
will die.
My fatigue demands no stress when it sends me to sleep mid-episode
and auto-play continues on. My light sensitivity imposes
curtains closed, lights off, screen brightness dimmed.

I select a soothing rhythm
of problems solved.
A quirky female-male pair investigating crimes over many seasons.
Women who can fight,
who can survive anything.
Series that pass the Bechdel Test.
Elementary. Bones. The Mentalist. Lucifer.
I watch each one from start to finish
and back to start, at .75 speed when possible.

I see nothing new, I feel nothing new.
The same shows from the past repeat,
over and over. The same mysteries are solved,
over and over.
Time has frozen.

I remember when I first saw these shows.
I was full of life at high speed, too busy to see every episode.
Out having fun, working late, traveling.
Connecting, contributing.

Now I float in a slow motion dream state.
In my dreams, these unstoppable, brilliant, fictional teams
solve my disease. They can handle anything,
why not this?
The spark of hope is a fantasy, a fairy tale.
But if writers are people
who can create these fantastical characters
and their intricate challenges,
there's gotta be people
who can create a resolution to my illness.
Right?

In the real world, weeks pass.
Months.
Seasons.
I am shocked
at glimpses that the world has moved on,
my friends' lives have moved on.
I am Rip Van Winkle, I am Sleeping Beauty.
I am a bear hibernating in a dank cave, I am a cicada
resting under the cool earth, I am a future butterfly's chrysalis
dissolving in a weather-ravaged cocoon.
What will the world be when they find a cure and I can wake up?
What will I be?

This Is What You Get

Mora Lee Mattern

Inspired by Radiohead's *Let Down* and *Karma Police*

Promise to think of me
Whenever the fog rolls in
Especially when the weather
Calls for unforgiving
Sunshine instead

Meanwhile
I'll be keeping time
By the moon
In my makeshift house
By the side of the freeway

An eyesore to some,
But a nest, a safe haven, for me
Until they tear it down
'Cause I'm "a criminal" —
"A lazy addict who gave up"

In their world

Traffic thumps and roars
Helicopters hover, unbearable
And you wonder why
I never asked
For your help

Call yourself my safety net
I'm too proud, too —
I-don't-know-what, I

Wanted to do it all on my own
Just like nature does

And like Thom sings
"One day,
I am gonna grow wings"
And lift up out of this
Graceless place

Fly away,
Disappear completely
Into the fog
Where they can
No longer see me

And only you will remember
My forest, my trees, my tries,
How I tried.
How the judges yelled "timber!"
Against all my best cries.

Yet once finally free,
Soaring high, I will see:
It wasn't me they feared
All along but their own
Evergreen egos and greed.

Goodbye My Sweet Boy

Grace May

My sweet boy turned angry old man.
Narcotics for his pain was torturing me.
Medications still keeping him alive.

Forced into watching my sweet boy die.
I want to experience all of the pain.
I need to feel my heart shattering.

Beep, beep, beep. Then silence.
What is going on?!...
Now only a monotone Beeeeeeeep!

Why?!
Why wouldn't they let me watch
Your last breath on the monitor?

Why?!
Why turn the monitor back on
After it was already over?

Gone forever was that exact moment
When I lost my son.
Ripped away from me suddenly.

Sorry, but that's not closure for me.
The last final insult to the mother.
Yes, I am still the mother.

OUR POEM

Elissa Mittman

Our poem
Remembers the joy
I felt
Playing with you
My dear niece
On a cold January day

While gray and dreary outside
Nothing but sunny warmth
Radiated between us

An imaginative afternoon of
Creating fantastical stories
Playing school with stuffed animals and
Drawing trees, volcanoes, and mermaids

Was enhanced by endearing comments
I want more time to play with Auntie
Come back and play with me tomorrow
Auntie and I need our privacy please

We bonded together
Hopefully for a lifetime

Many years from now
When my memory fades and
You can't recollect events
From age five
We can read our poem
Together
Recalling a special day

Intergenerational Healing

Carrie Monger

"I think the fear of disconnection can make us dangerous." (Brene Brown)

I didn't know she was behind me.
The realization was devastating.
Time would not rewind.
What have I done?
Panic, yes.
Fear, yes.
Shame.

No one can know. Wait, everyone needs to know. If everyone knows, then I am in control. Bury it or get out in front of it? I won't bury it. I'll tell the world. Yes, that's the pattern.
Control the narrative. Self-deprecation, yes!

"Self-deprecation can have unwanted consequences if it goes too far. It can become self-loathing and self-sabotaging. "(Google AI)

I can't calm down. My nervous system is overloaded.
I'm agitated, restless, I can't stop crying. My body wants to flee. My mind won't stop.
Self-hatred meditations on repeat.
I listen to them over and over.

"I believe that if we want meaningful, lasting change we need to get clear on the differences between shame and guilt and call for an end to shame as tool for change. "(Brene Brown)

Nancy offers me compassion. "Do you know you're not the only one?" You care so much. You are a good mom. A good person. A deeply feeling person who deserves love and forgiveness.

"Guilt is adaptive and helpful—it's holding something we've done or failed to do up against our values and feeling psychological discomfort" (Brene Brown)

Dr. Becky says I can repair this. I can do that. I will do that. I, of course, must and will do that.
Time will not rewind.
Panic, yes.
Fear, yes.
Sadness, yes.

Her innocence. Her vulnerability.
If she had not heard, it would have been better. Certainly.
If she had not felt what she felt, it would have been easier.
There is another way.

"RAIN is an easy-to-remember tool for practicing mindfulness" (Tara Brach)

Shame- Yes
Devastation-Yes
Panic-Yes
Fear-Yes
Cheeks burning-Yes
Tightness in chest-Yes
Throat constricted-Yes
Watery eyes- Yes
Sadness- Yes

Recognize what is happening.
Allow the experience to be there, just as it is.
Investigate with interest and care:
Nurture with self-compassion.
(Tara Brach)

Can I allow this to be? Just as it is?

I didn't know she was behind me.
The devastation.
The creeping shame.
I cannot rewind time.
What have I done?

Recognize what is happening.
Allow the experience to be there, just as it is.
Investigate with interest and care:
Nurture with self-compassion.
(Tara Brach)

What will I do?

I will RAIN.

Back to Water

Jin Soon Moon

Swim!
Aquatic therapy for stiff back
Prescription glares to challenge
Shallow to the fearful deep end

Float on back!
Trust the kick, leans on circular support
Look up at the ceiling, count the smudges
Water has your back

Tread! Sweats and palpitations
What buoyancy principle?
Easy, like riding a bicycle, sure
Pedal in zig-zag waves, crossing lanes

Never learned to bicycle
City childhood
Why risk honking danger?
When freely navigate through subways

Here, a chance to master both, apply
Water and the wild streets
Annoying scratches without broken bones
Cough up water but not drowning

Firmness always held the back, of cycle
Kicks become powerful, as the speed
Ageless, joyous splashing
Overpowers the nagging back

STRETCHING AND MOVING

Carren Oler

Stretching and moving

My shoulders crackle

And it felt good –

I didn't think it would,

So I did it again.

Am I sensitive

Because of the incessant rain?

I am dreaming

Of healing,

Like watching

Slow motion film.

When I awake

I take my pen to write down

The images I've seen.

It doesn't feel like a dream,

Rather a travelogue,

A catalogue of images.

To what does this compare?

These private thoughts –

They're runny

Like honey slowly

Dripping in my mind –

Sweet and sticky.

The bones crackle,

It's like spackle

Repairing the cracks

Within my brain.

Let me slowly

Rotate my head again....

En Plein Air

Helen Pagowska

Blue sky pulled taut
Like a sheet.
No creases
Or clouds
To take away the smile on my lips.

Sprinkled snow lies on the ground
Like flour on a baking board.
I lift a perfect circle of ice from my cat's water bowl.
Held up, against the light,
It transforms into a beautifully etched piece of glass.
I marvel at Nature's beauty.
The frosty whiskers of the shed door latch,
The fine white lines woven by a spider
Now coating the wall with exquisite graffiti.
Intricate patterns drawn all across the canvas of the garden.

A quiet meow, and
A nudge against my ankle,
Bring me back to reality.

And I shiver
As we both hurry back into the warmth.

You Are Complete

Josephine Palmieri

Sitting by the shore, the waves attempt to break the storyline I've created,
'You do not belong; you are not complete,' the story echoes every day.

The gentle waves implore me to release the myth I long ago accepted,
'You are not your thoughts; they are not real, watch them like clouds as
  each one floats away.'

'You are not smart enough, pretty enough, courageous enough,' the story
  continues on with might.

'The sky, the sea, the sand are real; they are part of you; you are part of
  them,' the waves repeat.
'You are a God particle made of stardust and flowing beams of light.'
'You are all you need to be; you are enough; you are complete.'

Churches, Say Amen!

Lauren M. Poteat

The beds are made and the sky is clear.

It's almost time for our first visit.

"Who will we see?"

Grandfather. You should be kind when you see him and laugh often.

Keeping with time, on to the next visit.

"Who will we see?"

A new neighbor. Make sure to step lively.

Quiet whispers, we're on to the next visit.

"Who will we see?"

An old friend. She's left church and is on her way to heaven.

Nurse? For those who don't believe, who would you say are the churches?

Well, the churches are the people.

You're a great ear assistant. Who would you say are the churches?

Oh, that's easy, the churches are the people who help.

An Ancient, Lost Language

Lynn Quinn

I can be strong like the wind,
yet gentle as a caterpillar.

I can be fierce as a bear,
with sharp claws,
used to pick berries of curiosity around me.

I can be calm as the rain,
peaceful notes on the eve of my porch,
a familiar song that jingles like home.

I can be fascinated by simplicity,
how a spider walks on the ceiling,
to defy gravity and sense of common physics.

I can be elegant as a dressage horse,
trained to prance and perform as expected,
to do as I'm told.

I can be open as a book,
one who's existed on a shelf for centuries,
scribed in an ancient and lost language.

I can be wild and free,
a leaf who waltzes in a Fall breeze,
guided by nature through intuition.

I can be patient as a flower,
to wait to bloom,
until the bud is ready,
hidden beneath the depths of Winter snow.

I can be.
The many me's.
I can be.

Me.

The Background

Stacee Ryan

The hurting.

The sadness

The fractured heart,

is healing.

The anger.

The insomnia.

The sensitive emotions,

are feeling.

The anxiety.

The tears.

The memories are

never fading.

The energy.

The realization,

that life is still

Moving on.

The joy.

The gratitude.

The grief shall always be

In the background of my mind.

The growing, the hope.

The epiphany.

Everything that is connected,

goes to infinity.

Reply All

Kristen Thomson Sheely

Should I even bother trying at this point?
You've seen me make the attempts:
taking a pause, taking a breath
benefit of the doubt, grain of salt
change of perspective
even
but,
every angle looks the same
no matter how I tilt my head
my eyeline never fails
I sit and stare and never blink
my eyes tear
(as they always do)
and I never blink
because I never want to lose sight of him

So I'm done trying, especially in the should-be
golden light of Fall
with its sunlight a willful sword,
sharp, clean
at the ready to cut a line from a to b,
a line from past me to now,
a line to mark any sense of congruency
a line on the page like this one
line after line like slashes on wrists
neat yet violent
lines that have been said before
perhaps
alternate lines in an alternate world

a script shuffled out of order like
slides in a carousel in an old projector
with a long burned-out bulb
I keep in the closet just in case
precious images only in memory —
images that are just in the holding now

So no
since you asked
I have not healed
nor have I learned how that word
even applies to me
and no, I am not strong
nor have I figured out any other way
to go about my day
I'm no one special
I'm someone who has no idea
how I got here
nor how to survive this
no idea what to do
no idea of anything, anymore
yet
what I want to do is talk about him
to you and you
and you
and tell you how confused and angry and
helpless and furious and sad and anxious and
how utterly guilty I feel
every day every hour every minute
knowing absolutely
that he should still be here
and knowing he isn't
and so I owe it to him

I owe it to him
no matter how much it hurts me
or how much it makes you uncomfortable
I owe it to him
to keep saying his name
(say his name)
tracing each letter
every slant, every curve
looking for meaning
clues
a riddle within
I'm sure of it
a brief history of loss in the cursive
he deserves whatever I have left, and he never
will not deserve everything
I have:
he is my son

Life in the Folds

Samantha Simons

What is smooth but a blank slate awaiting a story?

Thousands of scores from thousands of days,

A crumbled roadmap of mishaps and regrets.

I gather up my corners,

Tuck the dark parts inside,

And collapse into myself, into invisibility.

For even the freshest of creases from the most valiant of efforts,

Long to fall back into old folds,

Of the familiar marks life has left behind.

Smooth doesn't exist here,

Or anywhere.

Leave me to the process,

As shapeshifting is the seductress of hope.

Bend me in a new way,

Sit me on a shelf in the sun,

Whisper the wishes of faith,

In the next shape I'm to become.

Life's Music

Donna M. St. John

There's music all around the world. You need to listen closely; because music is not always from an instrument.

Newborn baby's gentle rhythmic breathing.
Rustle of crisp Autumn leaves as the wind blows.
A couple expressing undying love to each other.
Beating heart of a new transplant recipient.
Two countries feuding many centuries, come together in peace.
Kettle's piercing whistle for my morning cup of tea.
Honking car horns during rush hour traffic.
Crashing waves against a beach's jagged cliff.
A cappella singing of "Amazing Grace" at a hilltop graveside service.

Sometimes Life's music is the greatest with just complete silence....

Sun

Jack Tattersall

Sun 7:39

Crests the cloud

    Swell of ridges

Greyed in shadows

    Silhouetted

Sun rising behind

    Breaks its light

Through the thickness

    Frayed edge of broken

Edges

    Like a sheet draws back

Or forward

    Seams open between

To swell

    Ridges of cloud

Rolling in bands

    Threaded cross the sky

White valley

    Blue tints between

Tears

    Like seams ripped apart

Wind combs the clouds

    Wave after wave

Sent from the ocean

    Horizon line unseen

swell of cloud after cloud

    To cross

Pass under the sun

    Span the blue above

The bed cast light

    On the dark ridge

Ignite the green coral sea shell

Sun 8:05

    Slips through the threads

Clouds

    Like rippled water

Slips to lines of dissolution

    Frayed

The weave thins

Sun woven her rays

Between

    Cast below on a tree

Catches

    Silhouettes on branches

Patterns of leaves

    On car hoods

Cross white churn

    Dark glass

Patterns of the canopy

    The outline of things

Inside

    On interlock brick

The alley totally shaded

    Broken open

The weft taken

    Blue up above is revealed

Ocean of water

    Casting its disturbances

Below

    In streams of light beams

And shoal schools,

Play in the coral lace

Tinting shells, shards of

Porcelain, stucco ribs

Frosty Night

Connie Taylor

After Robert Haight's, *How Is It That the Snow*

The full moon hangs

over frost-covered trees

lighting bare limbs,

leaves lost to fall winds.

Today the air is still, no breeze

disturbs the clinging white crystals.

Night colors, black and white,

define the winter months

when green is banished.

And yet,

clasped in tightly curled buds,

the stark limbs hold green within,

protecting it until the sun returns

to release color into my world.

Lately

Sara Gómez Trillos

Lately
it's the SAT NAM mantras
which have kept my feet on the ground –
grass and
tiny yellow flowers between my toes
when the world goes dark despite the sun
and I cannot breathe
inhale despite the wind
and my heart beats without clear rhythm
and my thoughts are stuck despite the flow

I know the pattern

More grandeur than it should have
reality demystifies
but we ignore it
Stuck stuck stuck in the thoughts and
the inhales that don't actually inhale
the wind whistling outside and the short exhales
that prevent the gasps from gasping and the
pum-pu-pmmmmm of the heart
that we feel
and we hear
and we
tremble

And the world seems black
dark
Grey

what is it?

Despite the sun outside
brightness doesn't match my thoughts

Inner world in turmoil –
Is there any other world?

Whispering Words on the Wind

Kathy Why

I'm not a poet by any means

My words usually fall apart at the seams

Give me paper to rip, scissors and glues

That's the way I express my blues

But today was different as I looked up high

I whispered words to the wind & I watched as they flew up into the blue

Sky

I prayed for a miracle I prayed so hard

I prayed from my heart she'd have a new start

I prayed that someone would hear me to take away her pain

I prayed someone would hear me to take away the strain

I whispered my words but I wanted to shout

I wanted someone to hear & to let them all out

The grief & the tears were too much to bare

So I looked to the universe & sent them out there to share

Whispering words on the wind…

DRAW BREATH

Mag. Judith Wurzinger

Breathing,
Deeply, slowly,
Through the heart, state to rest,
Feeling coherence arising,
Soundness.

www.ingramcontent.com/pod-product-compliance
Lightning Source LLC
Chambersburg PA
CBHW070125230526
45472CB00004B/1426